2 MINUTES TO
Confidence

2 MINUTES TO
Confidence

Everyday Self-Care
to Inspire and Encourage

Corinne Sweet

STERLING ETHOS

New York

To Clara and Ross, for lending me your confidence when mine wavered. Thank you both.

STERLING
New York

An Imprint of Sterling Publishing Co., Inc.
122 Fifth Avenue
New York. NY 10011

ISBN 978-1-4549-4296-2

Distributed in Canada by Sterling Publishing Co., Inc.
c/o Canadian Manda Group, 664 Annette Street
Toronto, Ontario M6S 2C8, Canada

For information about custom editions, special sales, and premium and corporate purchases, please contact Sterling Special Sales at 800-805-5489 or specialsales@sterlingpublishing.com.

Manufactured in Slovakia

10 9 8 7 6 5 4 3 2 1

sterlingpublishing.com

Cover design by Andrew Smith
Cover illustration by Lylean Lee
Interior design by Ginny Zeal
Interior illustration by Andrew Pinder

MIX
From responsible sources
FSC
www.fsc.org
FSC® C022120

Contents

CHAPTER ONE

An Introduction to Confidence

Are you a confident person?

When you walk into any room, do you feel cool, calm, and collected, no matter what faces you?

Do you find it easy to meet new people and start up conversations?

Will you try anything despite the risk?

Are you relaxed about your body, whatever its size, shape, color, texture, and ability?

Do you ask people out and make friends without breaking into a sweat?

Can you stand up and give a speech at five minutes' notice?

What Is Confidence?

Put simply, self-confidence is our ability to believe in ourselves completely to meet life's challenges. It's also acting in a way that conveys this belief to others and leads to success. Truly confident people are flexible, don't mind taking risks, are hard to faze, and can deal with whatever is thrown at them. They will try something new, relish challenges, and don't panic at life's difficulties. Some people are naturally confident, but confidence can be learned and gained through life experiences.

How Confident Are You?

You've picked this book up for a reason, and you may well be wondering what on earth you could do in two minutes to boost your confidence. The answer is you can learn and use a great deal of fairly easy techniques to help boost your self-confidence for facing and dealing with all kinds of situations in life. The place to start is to ask yourself (and reply honestly): *"How confident am I?"* If the answer is "very" then great. But most of us will answer "not very" or "a bit" or even "depends." Most of us want to feel more confident but don't know where to start. This book will aim to give you some practical, simple tips and exercises to help you build and boost your self-confidence.

Negative Self-Talk

As a psychotherapist, I see many people who are struggling with their self-confidence. I work with them regularly to help them stop the negative self-talk that erodes their self-confidence. I strive to encourage them to build a positive sense of themselves through making small changes. I have also worked on my own self-confidence over the years, so I am going to share with you some of the things I think can really work if you are feeling low in the confidence stakes.

Self-Esteem

Self-esteem and self-confidence are often confused, so it's important to be clear about what they mean. Self-esteem is the general feeling you have about yourself. It's the attitude you hold toward yourself: one of uncritical self-love and concern. It is liking yourself, forgiving yourself, and holding yourself in positive regard. It is true that your self-esteem will grow as a natural by-product of becoming more confident. You will feel pleased if you reach a goal or accomplish something, and that feeling can lead you to liking yourself more: thus, your self-esteem will grow naturally as your confidence increases.

Introverts, Extroverts, and Ambiverts

In general, extroverts are those people who are most comfortable making contact with other people, while introverts might well find it harder to reach out, make new friends, or speak in public. Some of us have a mixture of introversion and extroversion, which is called being an "ambivert." While most introverts will be quietly confident about their knowledge and skills, extroverts might seem more overtly confident yet actually feel shy with people one-to-one. Thinking about how introverted, extroverted, or ambiverted you are will help you build your confidence.

Confidence in Two Minutes

In this book you will find short exercises to do in your everyday life to give you a quick boost and release stress. Some of the exercises are geared toward training your mind; others train both your body and mind. The exercises include simple meditation or mindfulness techniques and creative and fun ways to help you relax to give you a quick and easy tool kit to use when you feel a dip in confidence. The more you practice these exercises, the quicker you will begin to feel the benefits. Do them throughout the day, appropriately, and your confidence will build over time.

Affirmations
for Self-Confidence

Positive affirmations are an important part of building self-confidence. They work at an unconscious level, and the aim is to bypass your critical conscious mind. See page 54 for more on using positive affirmations for confidence.

FALL IN LOVE
WITH YOURSELF

Take a moment to look in the mirror or at a photograph of yourself.
Say in a positive tone, *"I am beautiful, charming, and I really love
myself."* You may feel silly or self-critical as you say this, but ignore
those negative feelings and thoughts. Repeat a least six times.
Take a nice deep breath, smile, and repeat six times more. Take a
moment to see how you feel.

MIRROR MIRROR

Look in a wall mirror and say to yourself (with a smile), *"My future
has never looked brighter."* Notice how you feel when you say it:
do you accept it, dismiss it, laugh, grimace, argue with it, etc.?
Ignore any negative responses and say it again with conviction and
a smile. Repeat at least six times. Do this several times a day and
note any changes in how you feel about yourself.

Self-Care
for Confidence

This book is about integrating self-care exercises into your daily life to boost your confidence. It is about becoming aware of yourself, of how you feel, and what you need. You need to know yourself well enough to stop and give yourself a boost when you are struggling. This is the essence of self-care: noticing when you are tense, overburdened, exhausted, worn out, wired, fed-up, or self-sabotaging—and learning to take a couple of minutes to relax, refocus, and do something positive for yourself.

Two-Minute Confidence Booster

A two-minute mental break will refresh and reboot your mind and body, and therefore your life. Research shows that doing this daily (and several times a day) will help reduce muscle tension, headaches, digestive conditions, and stress overall. You will increase your ability to tackle new tasks as you oxygenate your blood and brain. Endorphins, melatonin, growth hormones, oxytocin—the feel-good chemicals you get from breathing deeply and taking a moment away from stress—will help you feel calmer and more in control. Thus, a two-minute mental break can also help you face the next challenges of the day.

Establish Self-Care Habits

Self-care is not a last-minute add-on; it is absolutely essential and needs to be fully integrated as a practice into our daily lives. It needs to become a habit—like drinking more water or brushing your teeth. In fact, adding little acts of self-care into our daily habits is a very good way of learning to weave self-care into the fabric of each day: such as stretching while brushing your teeth or lying on the floor doing pelvic exercises while on the phone to friends. You just have to give yourself permission to do it. It's not a waste of time: it's essential and lifesaving.

Confidence on the Go

The beauty of a two-minute break is that it can be done anywhere and anytime. You don't have to be sitting in the lotus position in a spa. You can be sitting, lying down, walking, waiting in a line, in the back of a car, in a cab, on a plane, or train. You might be waiting for an interview, or on a couch, beach, bench, even in the restroom —in fact, anywhere (except when driving or using machinery, of course).

We all need to take mental breaks throughout the day. When you feel you've had enough, or are reaching "full" on the dial, consciously stop and do something else for a couple of minutes. With a little practice, this will form part of your self-care regime and will actually help you to get things done. Ironically, stopping and taking a break helps us achieve our goals far more effectively than doggedly pushing on through.

POWER STRETCH

Take a moment to stop what you are doing, especially if you are sitting at a workstation or rushing through your day. Find a private space. Stand, feet hip-width apart. Put your arms over your head and stretch up to the ceiling. Make a loud, guttural noise a like "Aaagh" or "Grrrr." Reach your right arm up, stretch while saying "Aaagh" or "Grrrr." Then repeat with your left arm. Repeat six times, then shake your arms and legs out.

Energizing exercise

RISING AND FALLING

This can be done sitting or lying down. Get yourself comfortable and turn off your cell phone. Close your eyes and bring your focus to the middle of your forehead. As you breathe in, think "*rising*," and as you breathe out, think "*falling*." Keep your focus behind your forehead as you breathe in and out. Let go of any sounds you hear and allow your jaw to loosen as you breathe. Drop your shoulders and feel your feet on the floor. Keep breathing, deepening the breath as you go. Take a few moments before you open your eyes and set off again.

Meditation exercise

CHAPTER TWO

Body Confidence

Ask yourself the following questions:

Do you like your body?
Are you confident about your appearance?
Do you spend a lot of time worrying about it?
Do you also spend a lot of time, effort, and money trying to perfect yourself?
Are you happy with your clothes and your look?
Do you criticize and compare yourself all the time?

What It Means to Be Body Confident

Body confidence is about being comfortable in your own skin. It's about liking your body, no matter what shape, weight, color, and height you are. It's also about being able to look at yourself, both naked and clothed, and liking what you see. Being able to say, "This is who I am and what I look like," while accepting your differences and imperfections. Being comfortable with yourself, just the way you are.

Body confidence is about turning off the critical, self-attacking voice that says you can't go to a beach, dress a certain way, or go to a party because you're not good enough. It's about thinking positive thoughts about your body and appearance, and not putting yourself down. It's also about not comparing yourself to others and finding yourself wanting. It's about saying, "I'm okay as I am," or even "I like the way I look."

The Pressure
to Be Perfect

We are living in an age when being perfect has never felt so important. A 2019 survey by the Mental Health Foundation found that one in five adults living in the UK are worried about their image on social media, with one in eight having suicidal thoughts because of it. While one in fifty Americans suffer from body dysmorphia, according to a 2020 survey from the US Anxiety and Depression Association. Studies have shown that parental influence is very important—if a parent has a negative relationship with their body, it's likely that this negativity will be passed on to their children.

Media Influence

Body image is a constant subject in the press, on TV, in movies, in advertising, podcasts, and on social media. Open the pages of many women's or men's magazines, and there you will find pages of text devoted to achieving the body beautiful accompanied by endless criticizm of the body shapes of celebrities and ordinary people. Yet, we are only human, and therefore flawed and unique, so the notion of being perfect is really impossible to achieve in terms of our bodies. However, the relentless 24/7 pressure of social media has made us all extremely aware of body image and led to us judging ourselves in very negative terms.

We can easily look at celebrities and influencers and wish we looked like them (although we don't have their wealth or team of dedicated helpers). We are also duped by impossibly altered images and pine self-critically for the perfection they seem to reflect. These influences are particularly damaging in our childhood, teens, and twenties when we are growing-up and forming a sense of ourselves. It is also hard as we age and compare ourselves to people who never seem to get old, as if they are lesser mortals: where are their wrinkles and wobbly bits?

Compare Is Despair

One of the most damaging aspects of body image
is the social pressure to compare ourselves with others.
In therapy, there is a notion of "compare is despair." In
other words, every time you look at a parent, sibling, friend,
colleague, or celebrity, and wish you were like them in some
way, you undermine yourself and your self-confidence. It is far
more important to be the best person you can be, and to
appreciate yourself for how you look and the body you have,
rather than compare yourself to others, and to impossible
(and even contorted) ideals.

BLOW A KISS TO YOURSELF

In private, take a look in a big mirror. You can do this with clothes on, or without. Look at yourself for a moment, and then blow a kiss to yourself warmly. You may feel silly, but smile and do it again. Try blowing several kisses and smiling as you do it. You can also do this with a small mirror in a restroom at work or when you are at someone's house and you feel nervous. It's a great way of boosting your confidence.

Practical exercise

Body Image and Body Dysmorphia

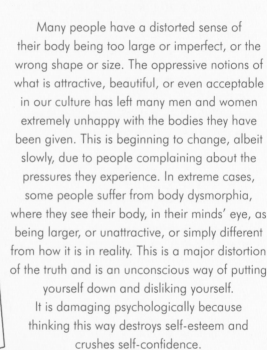

Many people have a distorted sense of their body being too large or imperfect, or the wrong shape or size. The oppressive notions of what is attractive, beautiful, or even acceptable in our culture has left many men and women extremely unhappy with the bodies they have been given. This is beginning to change, albeit slowly, due to people complaining about the pressures they experience. In extreme cases, some people suffer from body dysmorphia, where they see their body, in their minds' eye, as being larger, or unattractive, or simply different from how it is in reality. This is a major distortion of the truth and is an unconscious way of putting yourself down and disliking yourself.

It is damaging psychologically because thinking this way destroys self-esteem and crushes self-confidence.

POSITIVE HAND EXERCISE

Writing exercise

Take a piece of scrap paper and a pen or pencil. Put your hand palm-down on the paper with your fingers spread out. Draw around your hand with the pen or pencil. On the inside of the hand, write all the things you like about your body. Then on the outside of the hand, write all the positive things people have said to you about your body—as many as you can remember. Notice if there are any crossovers between what you like and other people say they like. Put this paper on your wall or carry it with you, so you can remind yourself of your good qualities when you feel less than good about your body.

Cosmetic Surgery and "Tweakments"

The quest for perfection has led to a rise in addiction to cosmetic surgery and "tweakments" (nonsurgical procedures such as fillers, Botox®, brow lifts, skin peels, and laser treatment). Women in particular are targeted for these treatments, especially via magazines and reality TV shows featuring cosmetically enhanced bodies portrayed as "the norm." Men, however, are increasingly spending on cosmetics and body enhancement procedures (such as hair replacement, fat reduction, and penis enlargement) to halt natural aging and to improve their apparent attractiveness.

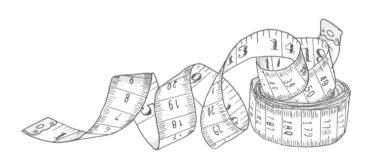

The Body Positive Movement

Because we are all different and unique, a "body positive" movement has grown internationally (mainly led by women), as a way of counteracting the quest for body perfectionism. This finally means that people with disabilities and of every size and color are beginning to be portrayed and promoted in the media and elsewhere. Even Barbie® dolls are changing to embrace disability and diversity. This is important to help people accept their individual appearance, shape, ability, and color, and to make being different acceptable.

Tattoos and Piercings

While body art can be a great way to express ourselves, it can be addictive, and for some people covering themselves from head to toe with ink and metal becomes an obsession. Before getting a new piercing or tattoo, take time to really consider what you are doing with your body as some body art is difficult and painful to remove. It can be a wonderful expression of personality or of belonging to a particular culture or group, but body art can also be a way of hiding our bodies. Learn to love yourself just as you are before getting a new piercing or tattoo, and always make sure it is done safely and hygenically and that you are sober and fully aware of the outcome.

Gender Identity

Over the past few years, there has been a lot of discussion about people questioning their assigned gender (male or female), and the fluidity of gender identity. How people define themselves sexually had been a big part of the body positive movement. There has been a great deal of personal sharing on social media, which has opened up the subject to a wide audience. However, this has also created an expectation of openness, with which not everyone feels comfortable. For some people, this can create more anxiety. It's very important that people have time to work out for themselves who they are and how they identify. Individual or group therapy can be a great help with this. Becoming confident about who we are, how we look, and how we identify is totally personal and may take considerable time to get clear. It's important to be patient with yourself and with the process.

YOUR BODY POSITIVE INVENTORY

Practical exercise

Find a private place with a mirror. Look at yourself in the mirror and take a few minutes to really see who you are. Turn off any negative or critical thoughts, if you can. Sit comfortably and ask yourself the following questions, noting the answers on your cell phone or in a notebook:

How do you see yourself?

Which groups do you belong to?

How would you describe yourself (white, mixed heritage, person of color, disabled, etc.)?

What is your relationship to your body and how does it affect your confidence?

Look at your answers and consider what kind of support, if any, you need to feel truly comfortable with who you are.

Quick Body Confidence Boosters

To improve body confidence, we need to give
up negative patterns of behavior and thought, and
instead adopt a warm, accepting stance toward ourselves.
We need to focus on learning to like and love ourselves
and our bodies, just the way they are.

Stop Comparing

If we stop comparing ourselves to others, our body confidence will grow. Accepting our bodies as they are and learning to love ourselves is key. To this end, don't put yourself down or make jokes about yourself or your body—it's important to treat yourself with respect. Put self-care at the center of your body maintenance, with a kind and caring attitude toward yourself.

Be Kind to Yourself

Groom yourself with love. Look after your hair, skin, teeth, eyesight, and appearance, and dress in a way that makes you feel good— create your own style, wear a delicious scent, and express your personality. Really care about your diet and put good things into your body, but try not to become overfastidious or obsessive about it. Adopt a healthy approach to food and drink, with nourishment at the center. Keep alcohol to a moderate level and avoid illegal drugs, which can damage your body and brain. Don't smoke as this is highly detrimental to your body, and be careful with painkillers, especially opioids, as it's easy to become addicted.

Treat Your Body Well

Exercise your body and find things to do with it that bring you enjoyment. Look after your health and attend to problems early (see a dentist, doctor, and optician for regular checkups). Use contraception to look after your sexual health and emotional well-being. Rest when you need (power naps can be great for this), and allow your body time to heal and repair itself.

The Female Lead

Being body confident does not necessarily mean flaunting our bodies, but it does mean loving and accepting who we are, warts and all. In recent decades, women have forged their way, gaining confidence in every sphere—sometimes a quiet confidence, or a cooperative confidence, or a competent confidence, and certainly, confidence borne of constant multitasking. Confidence is not just based on copying a loud, competitive male style or looking a prescribed way. Both women and men are experimenting with how they look and present themselves more than ever and gender boundaries are often blurred. Learning to be truly self-confident includes expressing ourselves in our own unique ways.

Practical exercise

POWER EXERCISE

Try this at home or in a private space. Sit on an upright chair, armchair or couch, and "manspread" your legs—sit with them wide apart in a confident pose with feet planted on the ground. Try taking up as much space as you can. Spread your arms out too along the back of the chair for greater effect. Enjoy the feeling. Revel in thinking of yourself as confident and powerful. Hold the pose for a minute or two. Relax and see how you feel.

Eating Disorders

Eating disorders, such as bulimia and anorexia, are deeply linked to feelings about body image (see pages 22–23). Sadly, eating disorders are on the rise among both men and women. Young people in particular are feeling the pressure, partly due to the use of social media and photo-based apps. It's not only the images on social media that cause distress among the young—it's also the comments section, where people are often abused or ridiculed because of how they look.

When to Get Help

Eating disorders arise when we don't accept or love ourselves. They are a form of self-punishment and are an expression of unspoken or unacknowledged pain and anger. Often they are a way of protesting at treatment or attitudes from others and can be a kickback against feelings of being controlled. Eating disorders can become a miserable preoccupation and a serious risk to health (even life). It is essential that sufferers get help as soon as possible from medical professionals to learn to accept themselves and improve their relationships with food. After all, food is what keeps us alive and shared meals are often central to our social and family lives.

Accepting Yourself Inside and Out

By putting so much emphasis on our bodies—their appearances, shapes, and sizes—we can feel like everything has to be judged from the outside. The most important part of body confidence is learning to love ourselves from the inside out. A building that is just held up by scaffolding would be wonky and unstable. But once there are strong inner structures to keep it upright, the scaffolding can come down, and the building can stand on its own and withstand whatever life throws at it.

Building
Body Confidence

It can be very easy to take our bodies for granted.
Our bodies are an exceptional piece of evolution.
Most of us can run and jump, move and dance, and climb and
swim. We can sing, play, and make love. Some can even create
and feed brand-new human beings.

Explore Your Body's Limits

Human bodies are a wonder to behold and explore. If you are a sporty person, you may be used to exploring your body and its abilities in all sorts of ways. However, many of us are desk-bound and overloaded with work, and perhaps don't use our bodies as much as we'd like. If you liked ballet or soccer as a child, perhaps you could return to it as an adult. You don't have to compete, but perhaps you can enjoy the experience of stretching at the barre or kicking a ball around with some friends, just for fun.

Try Something New

Some people enjoy extreme activities such as bungee jumping, kitesurfing, skydiving, or white-water rafting as a way of (literally) stretching themselves. They face fear, they explore their body's strength and abilities, and they achieve something new. Other people might explore new sports and gain new skills, such as learning to sail, snowboard, or rollerblade. Whatever you try, you should check with a doctor to ensure you are in good enough health, especially if you are returning to exercise after an illness or a long break, and if you have a disability, you need to think about your mobility and fitness levels. Learning a new skill or sport could be a real antidote to the stress of everyday life. Plus, it will give you confidence in exploring what your body can do. Exhilaration, self-confidence, and sheer pleasure will be your reward.

Use Your Voice

Exploring our voices or the musical abilities of our bodies can be very empowering. Joining a choir or an amateur theater or musical group can be wonderful for boosting confidence, as can learning an instrument and singing along. It's all part of getting to know yourself and how to use your body to its full extent. Research shows that the act of singing releases feel-good endorphins, and choral singers rate satisfaction with life higher than non-choral singers.

EXPLORING SOUND

Practical exercise

You can do this alone or with a good friend or partner. Stand in the corner of a room and if you are with someone, ask them to stand on the other side of the room. Think of a scale from one to ten in your head where ten is full volume, then think of a phrase like *"I'm alive,"* *"I'm happy,"* or *"I love my body."* First, take a breath and say the phrase at the volume level of one to three—this will be quite quiet. Then put your hands on your solar plexus, palms down, and try level five. See how that feels. Can you feel the vibrations? If you have someone with you, ask them what they heard. Then take a deep breath and try shouting the phrase at level eight to ten. Really project your voice across the room. Make your voice as loud as you can without straining. Did you experience the power of your voice projecting out of you? If you have someone with you, ask them what they felt when you used your voice to its utmost. See how you feel afterward.

CHAPTER THREE

Social Confidence

Socially confident people are able to:

Walk into a room and feel comfortable meeting new people.

Talk to complete strangers.

Stand up and give presentations.

Perform in public—music, dancing, singing, athletics, broadcasting, or drama.

Ask questions in front of others.

Take physical, intellectual, and emotional risks in public.

Try something new.

Face interviews and auditions.

Be with children in a positive, playful way.

Start a business or be an employer and effectively manage people.

Lead politically or in the business world.

Go on first dates.

Learn to Present Yourself

Most of us would like to be socially confident but are unsure how to achieve this. The idea of feeling relaxed and confident in social situations, and not worrying about making mistakes, may seem out of reach. However, it is possible to develop confidence about doing something in a social sphere, deliberately and effectively. It won't be an overnight job; it may take weeks, months, or even years, but with determination, experience, guidance, time, and a willingness to learn, you can succeed. You will need to be able to listen to feedback and learn to deal with criticizm and even rejection. However, if you do this constructively, it is possible to learn how to present yourself better in a social sphere, even if you are terrified at the thought.

Creative Visualizations

Creative visualizations are literally pictures you paint in your mind. It helps to have a good visual imagination, but all of us can imagine ourselves on a beach. Try it now—create the picture in your mind and see where it takes you. You can make a situation ideal or comic, or rerun something that was disastrous and turn it into a raging success.

These are useful techniques to reinvent in your mind how something might be done differently. Creative visualizations help you envision yourself as powerful or confident and can help change neural pathways in your brain if you use them regularly. They are a helpful tool in building both your self-confidence and self-esteem.

SEE YOURSELF SUCCEEDING

Find a comfortable spot sitting in a chair or lying down somewhere private. Close your eyes and imagine yourself in a situation you are dreading. "See" yourself as a confident person, knowing what to do. Approach people in your mind's eye, hand extended for a handshake or simply making eye contact. Imagine yourself as cool, calm, and collected. You are appropriately dressed and you feel confident. Smile in your visualization. You can do this with anything you are challenged by doing: giving a talk, making a presentation, going for an interview, or meeting someone for a date. See the other people or person as being pleased to see you. Replay this image in your head a couple of times. Open your eyes and see how you feel.

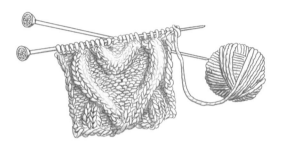

Practical
exercise

KNIT AWAY SHYNESS

If you feel shy in a social situation, nervous on the subway or bus, or worried about an evening out with people, take something with you to occupy your hands. You could take some simple knitting or crocheting, or string or thin rope to knot (sailing knots, macramé etc.). You can use your cell phone for instructive help, or learn a simple craft and take it with you. It may help you ease your way into the conversation, and people will be interested in what you are doing. You can teach them how to do it, and it creates a distraction from feeling shy or awkward.

SQUEEZE OUT YOUR STRESS

Keep a small stress ball in your jacket or coat pocket. When you are in situations that make you nervous, pop the stress ball in the palm of one hand and squeeze. Pummel and squeeze it when you are with other people, interacting. It can help ease your stress to push your feelings into the ball, especially as you speak. You could carry a stress ball to meetings or social interactions to help you through difficult moments.

Practical exercise

Nature Versus Nurture

Some people seem to be naturally more socially confident than others. It can be down to many factors: class, culture, gender, parental role models, educational experience, personality, as well as individual life experiences. Our backgrounds can play a strong part in how confident we are, alongside social and cultural learning.

Research by Corina Greven at King's College London and Robert Plomin of the Institute of Psychiatry found that women still have a biological tendency to avoid conflict and seek acceptance, while men tend to take more risks under pressure. Interestingly, the research concludes that academic self-confidence is 50 percent nature and 50 percent nurture—so we are somewhat hardwired on the social confidence front. Most psychological research shows that, typically, men tend to overestimate their confidence, whereas women tend to underestimate it.

TAKE YOUR OWN HAND IN HAND

If you are feeling anxious, shaky, or nervous before or during a social situation, try this. Put one hand face upward just in front of you and then clasp it with the other. Sit like this for a couple of minutes, just holding your own hand. Feel the strength of your hands clasped together. If you are standing up, you can hold them in front of you at waist height. Few people will notice this, as it is a common stance. Be aware of the feeling of your hands clasping, as it will boost your confidence. If you are feeling self-conscious about doing it, hold your hands behind your back but keep them clasped. This will send a message to your brain that you are not alone and is a great source of instant comfort.

Calming exercise

What Does Social Confidence Look Like?

True social confidence is not showy, bossy, or loud.
It is quiet, unruffled, solid, and unshakeable. It has power
and gravitas. Socially confident people appear comfortable
in their own skin, hold themselves well, and wear clothes
that say "this is me."

Social confidence is also the ability or willingness to take a risk,
look a bit silly, meet people without wearing makeup or
simply being yourself, warts and all. Some people feel
worried that they are not good enough and fear imposter
syndrome (see page 109), whereby they pretend to be better
than they are or are not what they seem. Being real means not
being showy or presenting a "case self" like a mask. It is about
being you and thinking you are good enough. Socially
confident people aren't afraid to let the cracks show and are
comfortable with their imperfections.

Practical exercise

BE A PEACOCK

If you usually wear a certain color or style of clothes, experiment with dressing up in something in private that makes you feel powerful. If you usually wear gray, blue, or black, try a new color like red, pink, orange, or purple. Try a power jacket, dress, or shirt that makes you "peacock" (you can borrow these or get something in a thrift store). See what it feels like to wear lovely fabrics, such as satin, velvet, or silk. Try a color you would never usually wear or a style that is strong—a tight dress, an evening jacket, tartan, or sequins. Try color on your hair (spray-on is fun) and/or try some bold makeup. Walk around your room in character and show yourself off in the mirror. Imagine yourself at a party or function dressed up like this. Experiment with what works for you.

Self-Consciousness and Social Anxiety

One of the major enemies of self-confidence is self-consciousness. It's the stuff of drama, poetry, and comedy. When we are very focused on how people see us, we are not really present to make contact with others. Introverted people, in particular, might find it difficult to meet new people or express themselves and can feel uncomfortably self-conscious in social situations.

Conquering Self-Consciousness

Social anxiety can be excruciating and can occur when shy people feel they have to struggle to start a conversation, do something unplanned, or be in the spotlight. It can cause a rise in heart rate as anxiety releases cortisol and adrenaline (a "fight or flight" panic response), and suddenly people find they are sweating and shaking with fear.

However, it is possible to conquer the self-consciousness that makes social contact so daunting. Gradual exposure to social situations, perhaps in the company of one good friend, a family member or a trusted colleague, can help you to be more relaxed. Also, preparation can help—working out what to say and when to say it can ease discomfort, even rehearsing with someone beforehand. It can also be useful to put your attention on the other people and prepare a couple of topics you might introduce as conversation. Having an interest in other people is a great way to prevent the spotlight from being on yourself.

As with all confidence-building issues, trying new things will help you move forward and is far better than shrinking back and saying, *"I can't do it."* Even if you sweat, feel shy, stumble over words, or forget what you are saying, the fact that you are trying counts for a lot. In time, you can learn to relax in company as you are exposed to situations that make you feel challenged. The more you do it, the easier it should get.

Practical Ways to Tackle Self-Consciousness

*End negative self-talk—stop putting yourself
down and telling yourself you can't do x or y.
Prepare—doing your homework will make you feel ready.
Put your attention on the other person and minimize
worrying about yourself as much as you can.
Find an ally and ask for their support.
Take two-minute mental breaks at social events to
release your stress, like a valve—step out from
the room, group, party, or meeting, and do an
exercise to calm yourself.*

CONFIDENCE-BUILDING BREATHING

When we are nervous, our breathing becomes shallow and we may hold our breath. Before or even during a challenging social encounter, try the following. Find a quiet space (the restroom, a corridor, in your car, an empty room, or subway carriage) and close your eyes. Focus on your solar plexus (the space just under your ribs). Put the flats of both hands on your tummy just under your ribs with your fingers touching. Lift up your breastbone slightly and breathe in from your belly. Feel the air come in through your belly and up to your lungs, then blow out of your mouth making a hissing sound or a "Ffffffff." Continue with this breathing for ten inhales and ten exhales. Feel your tummy go up and down under your palms. Open your eyes. See how you feel.

Body and Brain Reset

If you find it hard to speak up or have difficulty
making eye contact, you will need to reset your brain to
create a positive mindset. It is possible to do this, if you want
to, but it takes time. Changing a habit of a lifetime takes
commitment, experimentation, and repetition. You have to push
back against what feels habitual and try something new. To
do this, you have to become aware of what you usually do
and then do something different. Each time you push
back against what you usually do, you will reset your brain
and your body and it will get easier next time.

PUSH THE WALL

Try this if you are feeling nervous about an upcoming event, particularly if you are worried about feeling shy and self-conscious or becoming tongue-tied. Stand facing a wall (either at home or in an empty room) and put your palms flat against it. Then lean into the wall and push out. Repeat ten times. If you cannot be heard, try grunting as you do this. You can also try pushing yourself away from the edge of a table or desk a few times, again grunting as you do so. The act of pushing sends signals to your brain that you are fighting back, you are strong, and you can succeed. The exercise also helps release pent-up tension, allowing you to enter the situation in a calmer frame of mind.

Practical exercise

Positive Affirmations

Positive affirmations are a great way of boosting your social confidence. They plant a message in your brain that you are capable of doing something and help defeat negative self-talk, which is how we sabotage ourselves. Before entering a social situation that you know will make you anxious, it is a great idea to spend time preparing by repeating some affirmations to yourself in private. You can do this in front of a mirror, lying in bed, on the subway—in fact, anywhere. Your mind will begin to get the message and new neural pathways will be built as a consequence. Try these for starters:

"I am completely confident in every way."
"I belong."
"I am secure in my knowledge."
"I know just what to do."

Partner Power

You can practice saying one or all of the affirmations opposite (or one that really connects with you) with a good friend or trusted colleague. Accept that it will feel a bit forced at first, and you may giggle or feel silly or uncomfortable, but you need to persist. You will gradually plant in your mind some positive messaging that will help you become more comfortable in your own skin, and therefore become more confident in the daily social situations you face.

YES I CAN

Find a private space at work, in your car, at home, or somewhere outside. Stand up straight with your feet hip-width apart. Take a deep breath and say firmly and loudly, *"Yes I can."* Take another deep breath and repeat. Try saying it louder and louder each time, using your full voice and feeling the power surge through you. Do this daily to build your positive sense of self.

Affirmation

CHAPTER FOUR

Dating and Sexual Confidence

Going on first dates and forming sexual relationships can be a real test for our body, social, and sexual confidence. As social media has become a major way for people to communicate, we are relying less and less on meeting potential partners face-to-face. The ancient skills of catching someone's eye and flirting has been taken over by apps where a quick swipe decides a suitor's fate.

'Appy Dating?

Dating apps may seem fun at first, even liberating, but relying on them as a sole means of meeting a potential partner can be dangerous. We need to remember we are human animals, with sensitive sensory and physical equipment with which to form an opinion about others. As we spend more time relying on screens and apps, we seem to have less time to notice someone across the street, over the bus aisle, or in a room, and then linger over a coffee making conversation. Your new partner might be right in front of you, but would you notice if they were?

Learning to make eye contact, being able to strike up a conversation, being aware of people around us, and sensing if someone likes us are all dating arts that are rapidly dying due to us spending more and more time plugged into headphones and sitting head-down, playing online games or swiping on our devices.

Making Contact

We have become so aware of danger that making eye contact or speaking to someone you like directly almost seems like a problem. Obviously we need to be aware of our safety, and context is important (like where you are and who you are with). However, it is completely possible to smile at someone you find attractive, have a conversation with a complete stranger, hit on someone you like, and exchange contact details without putting your life in danger. It is a matter of judgement.

I am not suggesting for a moment you harass or stalk someone who does not reciprocate, but if we lose our ability to communicate one-to-one and only rely on technology for connections, we may potentially end up very deskilled in the communication arena. Being confident and friendly in your contact with others, and in finding new partners, is what makes life worth living.

TWO-MINUTE UNPLUG

If you travel on the subway or buses with your headphones on, head down, looking at your cell phone, try this. The next time you travel turn everything off, put your stuff away, and simply look around you. See what it is like to be in the moment, living in the present. If you make eye contact, see how it feels. Watch other people and what they are doing. Is there anyone around you find attractive? Would you be able to speak to them, if you wanted to? If you catch someone's eye, smile and see how it feels.

Practical exercise

The Dating Game

Ironically, we have never been so connected and interconnected, and yet at the same time we have never been so lonely. The whole dating game needs full participation, starting with you. Ask yourself:

What do I want?
What am I looking for?
What will I accept?
What do I have to offer?
What will I avoid?
Am I looking for casual encounters or a committed relationship?
What are my dating boundaries?

For your own sake, it's important you work out what you are looking for right from the start. This will put you in a confident position.

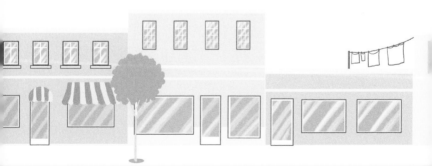

Learning to Trust

A fallout from the rise in using the internet to find a partner is the issue of trust. It's very easy for people to hide who they really are on a dating site, in terms of age or background history. You will need to take internet dating with a big pinch of salt and learn to use your instincts: if something feels wrong or doesn't add up, then trust your feelings. Be clear about your own intentions and ask any potential dates to be clear about theirs.

Take the Lead

Taking the lead and setting yourself a few rules
to follow are important for confident dating:

*For your safety, make sure you tell a good friend or family
member where you are going and when you intend to return.
Limit the amount of time you exchange texts and
messages, as meeting face-to-face will give you a clearer
idea of who the other person really is.
Limit the first meeting to an hour, over a coffee or a short walk.
Keep it simple and give yourself an easy escape
route if it doesn't work out.
Meet in the daytime in a public place.
Dress appropriately and don't go over the top to
impress on the first date—just be yourself.
Split the bill. It's good to keep things level right from the start,
and splitting the bill means things are equal,
and no one is beholden.*

After the First Date

If the date is good, give yourself time to feel and think about what you would like to do. If you want to see the person again, let them know. If you don't want to see them, be polite but clear. You can do this by message or text, or leave a voicemail if you can—it's more humane and respectful (unless you felt this would put you in danger). Getting to know someone gradually at a pace that suits you both is key.

Handling Rejection

No one likes to be rejected, but some people take it harder than others. If your confidence and self-esteem are already low, rejection can really make you despondent and can hit you where you already hurt. So what can you do? It's a good idea to prepare yourself when meeting someone new by thinking of it as an interview. You are effectively both seeing if the other person is a good "fit," and as with job interviews it may not work out. Not everyone likes everyone else—you won't like everyone you meet, and not everyone will like you. One of you may like the other more, and sadly that's life. However, when you both like each other enough to meet again it can be a big confidence boost. Try not to take rejection to heart. Dating is a bit of a lottery and a great deal of luck is involved. Try to keep an open mind and focus on sucessful dates, rather than any that don't go your way.

BUTTERFLY BLUES

If a date doesn't work out the way you want it,
you may feel anger, sadness, regret, disappointment,
or a mix of these feelings and more. Set a timer for two
minutes and allow the feelings to rise up in you. Imagine each
feeling as a butterfly and let it flutter up from your tummy up into
the air and away. Be aware of your breathing as you do this:
breathing in and out as steadily as you can. As each emotion
flutters up as a butterfly, let it go.

Confident Dating

It can be the case that women are still reluctant to ask men out on dates or will wait for the man to be the first to message or call. Of course, it's perfectly fine (and long overdue) for women to ask men out. In same-sex relationships, it is often a matter of delicate negotiation. It might be the more extroverted or experienced partner who feels more comfortable asking the other person out. Or maybe it's a clear mutual coming together. However, if you lack confidence in this area and are always waiting for the other person to act, you need to practice asking for what you want in other areas of your life. For your confidence to build, it's important to take baby steps toward success. Taking the initiative is a good place to start.

SPIRAL STAIRWAY TO SUCCESS

Visualization

If you are holding back from telling someone you like them, try the following creative visualization. Get comfortable in a chair or lying down and close your eyes. Imagine a golden spiral staircase winding up to the clouds. At the top of the stairs the sun is out, the birds are singing, and the sky is blue. See yourself at the bottom of the stairs, in the darkness, and take one step at a time up toward the top. As you take each step, feel the sun falling on your shoulders and face, and envision the blue sky above. When you get to the top, the person you want to ask out is standing there smiling at you. Hold out your hand and take theirs. Take the last step and walk toward the sun and blue sky together. Open your eyes and see how you feel.

Sexual Confidence

Becoming sexually confident does not happen overnight. From our teens onward, we are experimenting, experiencing, and working out what makes sense for us sexually. Several key factors contribute to building sexual confidence and how confident we feel between the sheets can alter over time. A key factor is knowing ourselves and being able to communicate our desires to our partners. This is not only especially important in a new relationship but also as our bodies change due to age, hormones, illness, or pregnancy. Something that worked for us in our twenties may not give us pleasure in our sixties, and it's important to understand and be able to communicate this. Read on for some key areas to focus on if you want to be more confident sexually.

No body is perfect. Sexual confidence has nothing to do with having a perfect body—it's how you feel about yourself that matters. There is a "cult of perfection" that makes us all feel unattractive in some way, but nobody is perfect and loving your body just the way it is is the only way forward.

Know your own body. Exploration of your own body is essential to having sexual confidence. When you know what gives you pleasure, how you like to be sensual, and what works for you, you are in a powerful position with a new partner.

Communicate. Being able to communicate what you do or do not like is crucial to gaining sexual confidence. Feeling that you have the right to say *"No, I don't like that"* or *"Yes, could you do that more"* is very important.

Listen to your partner. Knowing what they like, what they want, how they like to be touched, and pleasured is very confidence-building. It's great to feel you can be a satisfying lover.

Understand your pace. Some people like to go very fast; others enjoy a slow feast. If you understand your own pace (and sometimes it's a mixture of both), you are in a much better position to take charge of what you want sexually.

Mutual consent. Consent is important in all things sexual. If you are exploring sex games, using toys, or watching porn, make sure the other person is comfortable and happy to do so. Sexual confidence can build from exploring, but also from saying "no" and being respected. Sometimes people feel coerced into experimenting— only do so if you really want to.

Look after your sexual health. It's extremely important to make sure you take care of your contraception, don't rely on a partner to have condoms (always have your own), and you have regular health checks. Make sure you are checked for STIs, HIV, or pregnancy, if you have unprotected sex.

Have sex awarely. Minimize alcohol and drugs so that you are really present with someone. You might enjoy a drink during seduction (it does make people less inhibited), but having sex drunk is not particularly pleasurable or safe. Use your body with awareness and treat yourself well.

Dress up to feel sexy. Some people like to wear sexy underwear or slinky, silky clothes to make them feel better about their bodies. Anything that builds your sexual confidence is worth trying.

Bathe or shower with your partner. Lather each other's backs and wash each other with luxurious body wash or soap. Enjoy feeling and enjoying each other's skin and limbs. Avoid genitalia and erogenous zones—make it a sensual experience rather than a sexual one.

Imperfect sex. Sex seldom goes perfectly, so learn to deal with mishaps and laugh with (not at) your partner. Be relaxed if things don't work out for you both—there's always another time or another partner.

Enjoy soft sex. There is often too much focus on penetration and men often feel a lack of confidence as a consequence. Enjoy playing with toys and pleasuring each other with your bodies. Try new things like massage and explore. Your confidence will build if you are not too focused on traditional sexual play.

Share massages. Use almond-based oils, scented to your liking (sandalwood, cedarwood, and ylang-ylang all have arousing aromas). Ask your partner to lie on their front on a towel on the bed, couch, or floor. Smooth oil on their shoulders, back, arms, and buttocks. Stroke and massage gently, focus on digging your fingers gently into taut muscles to relax them. Turn your partner over and continue a full body massage along shoulders and arms, chest/breasts, solar plexus, thighs, legs, ankles, and feet, avoiding the genital area. You can also massage the head and neck, sitting behind them. Do this slowly and gently, then switch.

Accept your sexual identity. Some people feel wracked by wondering about their sexual identity and defining themselves. You may need to experiment and try things out. Just stay focused on what feels right for you, and be respectful of the other person, too.

PAMPER YOURSELF

If you have a couple of minutes after a bath or shower, take some lovely smelling oil or body lotion and anoint your body. Watch yourself in a mirror. Turn off your mental critic and stop any negative thoughts about your body. Feel the lotion or oil sinking into your skin and feeling softer and smoother. Feel the curves of your body and enjoy the sensations. Pamper yourself for a couple of minutes this way and think or say to yourself, *"I treasure my body and the pleasure it gives."*

Relaxing Exercise

LOVE YOUR BODY

Affirmation

It's easy to be negative about your body, especially if you have been teased, your weight has altered, you have had an illness or a disfigurement, or you have recently had a baby. This is just cultural pressure; plus you need time to get used to the new you. Take your clothes off in the privacy of your own home and stand in front of a mirror. You can just look at the top or the bottom, or all of yourself in one go. Try saying *"I like the way I look"* as you look in the mirror. Find at least three things you like about your body and enjoy looking at and touching them. Repeat *"I like the way I look"* as often as you can, and this will begin to improve how you view yourself. Self-acceptance is all.

CHAPTER FIVE

Relationship Confidence

Being confident in our relationships is an emotional challenge for many of us, yet it is essential for being able to have a happy life with someone. We constantly relate to a wide range of people: family members, friends, neighbors, colleagues, partners, children, and complete strangers. For the purpose of this book, this chapter will focus on romantic relationships.

Confident Relationships Start With You

Our relationship confidence is molded by our backgrounds and our cultures, and then shaped by our life experiences. Most of us want to form healthy, satisfying, and mutual relationships, and yet doing this can be complex and difficult. With almost half of all marriages breaking down, finding a partner for life can feel daunting. To gain confidence when building relationships, we need to gain confidence with ourselves first and foremost.

Being Yourself

When dating, many people try to be what they think the other person wants them to be as a way of trying to establish a new relationship. This seldom works, as we can end up being inauthentic and find that it's hard to keep up the charade. This can also lead to imposter syndrome (see page 109). So, it's important to be yourself and learn to be confident about being you if you are to build confident relationships.

RELATIONSHIP MAP

Draw a circle in the center of a piece of paper and write "me" inside the circle. Draw lines out from the circle and write the names of people who love you (friends, partner, family etc.). You can draw the lines and names in different colors, such as red for friends, pink for a partner, green for family. Make the length of each line equivalent to how close you feel to each person (so a short line to "me" means close, a longer line means more distant). When you are done, look at your map and acknowledge your relationships.

Writing exercise

Relaxing
exercise

FLOATING BLISS

You can either do this exercise for real in a swimming pool or as
a creative visualization lying in bed or on a couch. If in water, make
sure you are safe and use floats if needed. Close your eyes and
float on the surface of the water. Put your arms out wide. Imagine
yourself in a beautiful place, such as a meadow or the seaside.
See yourself lying in the grass or on the sand, relaxed and calm.
Just float. Enjoy the sensation of being free, calm, supported,
and serene. Breathe deeply.

Knowing Who You Are

Successful relationships are more likely to develop if
you know and accept who you are. When establishing a
new relationship, it is easy to hope that somehow the other
person will read your mind and understand you automatically.
Unfortunately (or fortunately), understanding comes down to us
being willing to educate the other person about who we are. It
takes time, patience, and persistence to reveal who you are,
what you like and don't like, how you think and feel, and
what you need and want. This is crucial for establishing
a healthy, confident relationship right from the start.

Work Out What You Want in Life

It's much easier to be your true self and to be happy with someone else, if you know what you want in life. Even if you haven't worked out the details, it's good to express where you think you are going as clearly as you can, so the other person is not in the dark.

Be Authentic

Being authentic is a huge part of knowing and being confident with yourself. Be your true self—your "best" self but not your "ideal self." You don't need to pretend to be better or different than you are: owning up to foibles and mistakes is better than hiding things. Keep it real.

HEART FULL OF GOOD

Draw a large heart (in color if possible) on a scrap piece of paper. Using a different color pen, write down words you associate with your positive personal qualities: "caring," "funny," and so on. Add words inside the heart every time you think of one. Keep it with you so that you can remind yourself regularly that you have very good qualities.

SELF-ESTEEM BOOST

Take a moment to look in the mirror and smile at yourself. Put your hands, palms down, over your solar plexus (the soft place under your ribs), and say with warmth and affection, *"I am totally lovable."* Repeat six times. Mean it. Keep smiling as you say it. See how you feel.

FIND YOUR "NO"

Find a space in private. Practice saying "no," first quietly, then at medium volume, then shout it loudly and confidently. Say it with feeling and release any anger. Try stomping your foot as you say it. Shout it if possible. If you are feeling angry, take a cushion, or pillow, and shout "NO!" into it very loudly. Practice saying "no" as often as you can. It will boost your confidence for saying it when you really need to.

Empowering exercise

Pleasing
and Appeasing

Being a people pleaser is a relationship killer. It's important not to second-guess your partner or put them first to your own cost all the time. This only leads to resentment and disappointment long-term, plus they may feel swamped by you. Pleasing someone all the time is actually a form of control, and we can't really control others. It's also impossible to make someone love you. Love has to grow naturally out of mutual respect, enjoyment, care, and communication.

Being a Rescuer

Allow your partner to struggle with things and work things out for themselves. Be supportive, but don't take over or belittle them. If you sort things out for them all the time, and "rescue" them endlessly, you may well end up feeling resentful and distanced. You will also infantilize them, so they don't grow and feel capable themselves. They may also end up resenting you.

Aspire Together

Research shows that there is something called the Michaelangelo Phenomenon, where we tend to develop into our ideal selves when our partner has the traits that we want to have for ourselves. We need encouragement, and we also watch our partners as role models of what we aspire to.

Handling Criticism

Being critical or "nagging" in a relationship eventually creates
negativity. It is controlling behavior and common to both sexes.
A "don't do this or that" attitude creates a constant feeling of
being in the wrong on the part of the person being
criticized. It is horrible to feel constantly judged and erodes
self-confidence. Relationships need to be managed
mutually, not controlled by one person alone.

If You Are the Criticizer

You may have a desire for perfection and feel uncomfortable in your own skin, hence needing to be critical all the time. You possibly had a critical parent or teacher who made you feel you were never good enough and are now unconsciously repeating this behavior. You need to learn to hold back from criticizing as it may ultimately push your partner away.

If You Are Criticized

It's a horrible feeling to experience somebody bearing down on you all the time, finding fault, tripping you up and testing you. It will undermine your self-confidence terribly, and you will begin to store up anger and resentment. You will need to find a way to say *"I would like you to stop criticizing me"* to your partner. It is a negative habit that will destroy your self-esteem.

Think Positively

For a relationship to be successful, both partners need
to focus on positive qualities in themselves and the other
person. If the relationship is established, this may involve
remembering the things you liked about the other person in the
first place, including what you admire. Also think about the
things you like about yourself. Couples reflect one another, and
if you are constantly focusing on the negative, the goodwill in
the relationship will fade. Constant doubting and second-
guessing are draining; negative behaviors—focusing on the
positive, of what you like and what you enjoy,
will help boost confidence.

Practical exercise

BACK ROLL

Try this exercise if you need to step away from a situation for a moment. Stand with your feet hip-width apart and let your hands hang down by your sides. Keeping your knees soft, slowly let your head move forward and tuck your chin in, then continue rolling your spine down until your hands are nearly on the floor. Gradually come up, unrolling your spine vertebra by vertebra, until you are upright again. Repeat this three times. Breathe in and out deeply three times. Relax.

Appreciate Each Other

It is important to appreciate your partner and be appreciated in turn. It's all too easy to take each other for granted. Say "thank you" and mean it when someone does something for you. Appreciate the small things your partner does for you, and if they take you for granted, ask them for some appreciation in return without criticizing or complaining. Try exchanging three things a day you appreciate about each other. You both deserve it. This builds a good feeling in the relationship as no one likes being taken for granted.

Importance of Trust

This is a big one for most people. Lack of trust comes from being hurt in previous relationships and shows where you are still hurting. Some people from very damaging backgrounds find trust almost impossible. As this is borne of our own insecurities and causes hurt, we need to heal so we can begin to trust others. Constant doubting, mistrusting, and questioning can be extremely corrosive in relationships and pushes others away. It creates a toxic atmosphere, which usually destroys the relationship.

MUTUAL APPRECIATION

Ask your partner to do this with you. Sit comfortably and take it in turns to say something you appreciate about each other. One person starts: "[name of partner], I appreciate the way you...[make me a coffee/cook dinner/rub my feet/clean up]," or something similar. Then, the other person says: "[name of partner], I appreciate the way you..." Try to just listen to each other's appreciations without making comment, laughing, disagreeing, or getting into a discussion. Just listen and receive, noticing how it feels.

Practical exercise

Handling Conflict

It is a common misconception that a good
relationship is conflict-free. Not so. Conflict is an
essential part of a relationship as two different people with
different ideas and feelings about things will inevitably clash at
times. Learning to handle conflict confidently and without
hurting each other is essential for relationship happiness.
Remember the three Cs for sucessful relationships:
communication, cooperation, and compromise.

Admit your mistakes. It's easy to become rigid or take up entrenched positions and fight about who is right or wrong all the time. This can be very wearing on your relationship. If you are in the wrong admit it, then say sorry and move on. Learn to forgive.

Listen to your partner. Really listen without interrupting, arguing back, or defending yourself. When we are angry, we talk over each other or assume we know what the other is going to say. Cool off and then take turns listening to each other without interruption or comment.

Don't apologize for everything. This may seem like it contradicts to the first point, but it doesn't. Sometimes we are too ready to appease, please, and apologize, even if there is no reason or if you still feel annoyed underneath. Feel confident enough to stand your ground without being aggressive. Be assertive.

Tackle the areas of conflict. If you know something isn't working for you, tackle it. Not by blurting it out, sulking, or shouting, but by deciding you need to say something about how you feel. Talk to friends or a therapist first and rehearse what to say. Find a way to express what you need—write it down even. Avoidance doesn't work long-term, as any issues always come back and need airing.

Blame Game

When you blame the other person, you are being
a victim. Blaming is a form of passive-aggressive attack
and rapidly wears out a relationship. It undermines individual
confidence. When someone is blamed and interrogated, it can
make them very resentful and angry. Even if they seem to
be a doormat, they may well be seething inside, which
is bad news for a relationship long term.

If You Are the Blamer

Ask yourself why you need to behave this way. What do you get out of it? Blaming is persecutory behavior and turns your partner into a punished victim. It is also a refusal (on your behalf) to take responsibility for yourself. You need to stop being destructive and move on.

If You Are Blamed

Being blamed can undermine your self-esteem and confidence, and make you feel trapped. Underneath those feelings, you may also feel very angry. Don't allow yourself to be blamed, and learn to speak your truth: *"I don't like it when you speak to me that way"* or *"I'd like you to stop blaming me for x or y."* The blame game gets nowhere and destroys relationships in the end—don't enter into it.

Self-Esteem in Relationships

Being confident in yourself and having high self-esteem
is one of the best ways of making a relationship work. It's an
old adage, but you can't love others unless you love yourself
and having low self-esteem can be a destroyer of relationships.
High self-esteem is crucial for making relationships work. If you
feel negative about yourself and don't love yourself, you will
find it hard to feel positive about your partner or love them.
Negativity infects each person in relationships. When you are
constantly putting yourself down, you become immune
to compliments or loving comments. You
brush them off, and at the same time
brush your partner off, too.

Be vulnerable. Research shows that real intimacy can be built when both partners are willing to open up and be vulnerable. Being titanium-coated is not attractive as it does not allow your partner to get close. To be vulnerable is to be human; to be human is to able to love and connect.

Learn to enjoy your own company. Confidence in relationships comes from being able to do things on your own.

Have your own interests. Some people believe that you have to do everything together—not so. Find your own interests and hobbies and enjoy them independently from your partner.

Value yourself. Don't put yourself down or use negative language about yourself. Treat yourself well and don't abuse yourself, especially with alcohol, drugs, food, and other addictions.

Look after yourself. Take care for your mental and physical health and well-being. Nurture yourself and get checkups from professionals when you need to.

Allow your partner space. You don't need to be with them 24/7 or to monitor their every move. Don't be envious or jealous of what they do without you, who they talk to, or what they enjoy —applaud their independence and that they come back to you fulfilled.

Self-Care for Relationships

If you care for yourself and look after your own welfare, you will show your partner that you are independent and can take responsibility for yourself. Looking after your physical well-being, fitness, diet, and mental health are attractive qualities as this demonstrates high self-esteem, which is very enticing. This puts you in a better position to have a mutually satisfying relationship from a place of confidence.

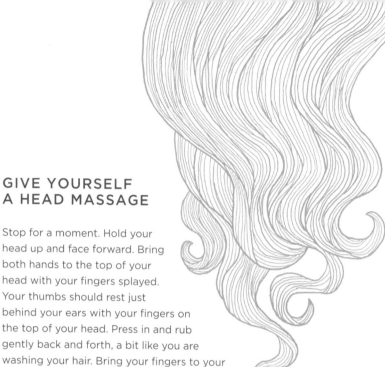

GIVE YOURSELF
A HEAD MASSAGE

Stop for a moment. Hold your
head up and face forward. Bring
both hands to the top of your
head with your fingers splayed.
Your thumbs should rest just
behind your ears with your fingers on
the top of your head. Press in and rub
gently back and forth, a bit like you are
washing your hair. Bring your fingers to your
forehead and temple and rub across your
brow and down the sides of your
head. You may find yourself yawning—allow the yawns
to happen. Rub for a couple of minutes then stretch
your neck. Breathe.

Relaxing
Exercise

Confident
Relationship Model

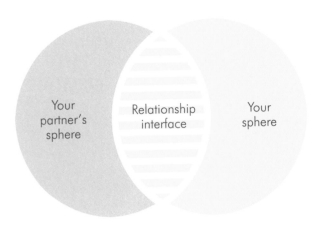

Relationship Interface

Think of your relationship as two overlapping circles. One circle is yours; the other is your partner's. You have your own life, work, concerns, interests, and passions in your circle; your partner has theirs in their circle. Where the circles overlap is where the relationship meets. This relationship interface is where you exchange ideas, interests, thoughts, and information—this is what keeps your relationship alive. Allow each other space to live, work, and relate in your own spheres, meeting confidently in the middle where you can be together as two separate individuals. Give up thinking the other person makes you whole or that together you are one. Believe instead that you are already whole on your own.

This confident relationship model will make for a longer, more satisfying experience. The romantic notion of being completed really disguises the dysfunctional "urge to merge." We need to be separate and be independent to relate to others effectively.

Confident Intimacy

Many people are terrified of letting somebody in or allowing themselves to be close to others as they fear getting hurt or being known intimately. This is usually down to negative past experiences. Being confident about yourself and having high self-esteem allows you to let people in (the ones you choose, anyway) and to be close to others. It can be very satisfying if you can take down any defenses built out of hurt and allow yourself to get close to someone. Intimacy is like a dance between couples—it takes time to learn the steps, and it might be two forward and one back, or even one to the side. However, intimacy is emotionally satisfying and crucial for a good sex life.

CHAPTER SIX

Work Confidence

Many of us spend most of our lives at work.
In fact, we probably spend more time at work than we do
sleeping, so it is very important to feel self-confident about how
we earn our living. In the current climate, which has seen a
drop in permanent work and a move toward short-term
contracts, part-time work, and self-employment, it is definitely
worth developing a self-confident attitude. Confident people are
more resilient and able to survive difficulty and uncertainty,
so they also succeed better longer-term.

Why Do We Need Work Confidence?

Developing and maintaining work confidence is essential for:

Getting work in the first place—applying, interviewing, dealing with rejection and other setbacks.

Learning on the job and keeping jobs.

Negotiating contracts, pay, and conditions.

Making requests such as flexible hours, a change to working conditions, maternity/paternity leave, and mental health support.

Engaging with interviews, reviews, and assessments.

Developing your role as you progress and/or are promoted.

Handling conflicts, disagreements, or complaints.

Deciding to look for a new job or move in a different direction.

Self-Esteem and Work

If your self-esteem is low, you may find yourself applying
for jobs that are unchallenging or unrewarding. Working
on building your self-esteem and self-confidence will help you
to think bigger about yourself, take risks, and face new
challenges. Many jobs demand that we learn new skills or try to
do things outside of our comfort zones. Your self-esteem and
sense of self-worth will grow each time you learn something
new or succeed at a task. Even if you make mistakes or mess
up, you can see it as a learning opportunity.

TONGUE STRETCH

Try this if you need to take a quick break at work. You can do this discreetly at your desk or workstation, or watch yourself in a mirror. Put the tip of your tongue behind your bottom front teeth. Push your tongue forward and let your jaw relax. Your tongue should flop a bit forward. Notice the sensation of your tongue behind your teeth and your jaw relaxing as you push it forward.

Energizing exercise

Calming exercise

TAKE A MOMENT

We spend so much time rushing around being preoccupied or screen-watching. Take a moment to stop the next time you are waiting for a bus or on the subway, or in a line, and bring your attention to the present. What do you see? Look at the people around you, notice their faces and clothes. See the trees, the sky, and the colors in your environment. Put your attention on the now just for a minute or two and take everything in. Breathe deeply three or four times, before moving on.

Self-Care at Work

Many of us feel driven to prove that we are worthy of employment by jumping at every request (reasonable or unreasonable) that is thrown at us at work. We might even find ourselves doing something risky or dangerous because our employer has told us to or has demanded it. We seem to believe that hours spent working are equivalent to productivity. Most of the research shows that our productivity actually goes down the longer we stay working—the opposite of what we seem to think. So self-care is hugely important to maintaining well-being while working.

Physical and Mental Health

Self-care at work is essential for maintaining good physical and mental health, both in and out of the workplace. Be sure to:

- *Take regular breaks.*

- *Make sure your workstation or your working conditions are appropriate.*

- *Eat healthy food and drink water regularly.*

- *Ensure you have the correct protective equpment, if necessary.*

- *Stick to specific hours—you should not be expected to work all hours without a break.*

- *Have access to natural light (or breaks outside).*

- *Report any bullying or harassing behavior.*

EAT AWARELY

Practical exercise

We often rush our food, gobbling it down while we're on the go or at our desks. Food should to be eaten slowly and savored—it's very unhealthy to eat on the run or in front of screens. Try putting your food on a plate, arranging it nicely, and taking smaller portions. Chew slowly and taste the flavors. Notice when you are full (we seldom finish everything on our plates when eating awarely). Stop when you have had enough and save the rest for later or share with someone. Enjoy feeling satisfied.

Build Your Work Confidence

As well as being a source of income, work preoccupies
us and gives us status and purpose. Many of us fall into a job
or jobs and are not sure whether it's really what we want to do.
Remember that you can always change track or retrain, and you
may want to have some sessions with a life coach or therapist to
help you work out your next steps.

You might work for yourself or decide to launch a
business. Again, it is important to get some guidance and
support when you are taking a leap into the unknown. Many
students come out of college with great qualifications and little
work experience, so beginning to climb the ladder can seem a
heartless slog. Internships and part-time work can
be soul-destroying, so what can you do to help yourself
build your work confidence further? Read on to find out.

VISUALIZE YOUR SUCCESS

Get comfortable in a chair, on the couch, or in bed. Close your eyes and imagine yourself doing the job you would really like to do. See yourself in detail: your clothing, your stance, and your situation. Envision yourself in the right surroundings, doing work you really like, being applauded, or cheered. See your success in your mind's eye. Beginning to think of yourself doing what you want is half the job of getting there for real. "See" this picture of yourself as often as you can—it will help build your confidence.

Prepare to Succeed

When looking for work or entering a new field, do your homework. Make sure you read up on what is needed. List your skills and work out what you need to know. Put yourself on a course or learn some new skills, if you need them. Do some unpaid work to get experience, or volunteer. You will gain confidence once you have hands-on experience of the field you are interested in going into. However, always prepare and know your stuff, as much as you can, for interviews. It always shows.

Be honest about yourself and your experience (or lack thereof). Be clear on your application or resume—keep it short and to the point. Know your strengths and weaknesses. Confidence comes from knowing what you can and can't do, what you like and don't like. You will come across to employers as much more employable if you are straight about these things. Self-knowledge is power in the workplace.

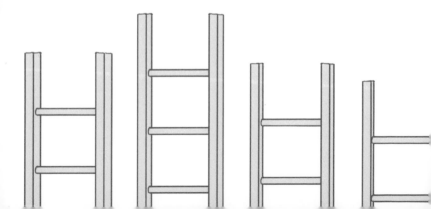

Aim High

The best way to conquer fears at work is to aim high. Many people fear that they will be caught out or feel overwhelmed, but with support and training, and taking baby steps, it is possible to achieve much more than you might believe possible. This is a real confidence builder. Women, in particular, tend to aim lower than men (men tend to overestimate their worth, skills, and abilities, whereas many women underestimate theirs). If you aim high, you will probably achieve much more than you thought possible —certainly more than if you aim low. This will boost your work confidence to no end.

Many of us experience imposter syndrome, where we fear we are not really what we seem to be and fear being found out. You might well feel out of your depth at work, but sometimes this is a good thing. Some employers will spot your potential and ask you to take on more responsibility or cover for someone. You may feel you are unqualified or inexperienced, but if you act "as if" you are good enough, you will probably end up good enough or even better. "Fake it 'til you make it" is the name of the game and can be a great confidence booster.

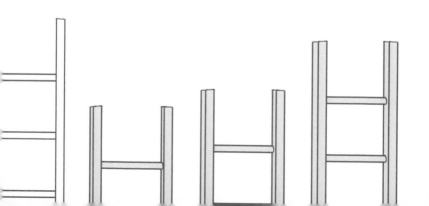

Be Assertive and Positive

Many things may annoy you at work, or you may feel overlooked for promotion or opportunities. It is important to learn to speak your mind, firmly and appropriately, but not be aggressive. Knowing the difference between being assertive and aggressive is important for success. Speak up if you feel overlooked, but in an appropriate way, so your colleagues can hear what you say. Ask for what you want or need, but do it with a level head (neither complaining nor being a doormat in the process).

Turning any negatives into positives will build your confidence at work. Instead of thinking *"I can't do that,"* think *"I can try."* Instead of thinking *"It'll never work,"* think *"How can I do this?"* We spend a lot of time and energy focusing on the negative at work, when focusing on the positive will get you further and enable your confidence to grow. Employers and colleagues like to be around positive people, too.

PEEL AN APPLE

Take an apple, and starting at the top where the stalk is, carefully peel it so that you get one long strip of peel. Keeping the knife or peeler near the surface of the skin, peel slowly, turning the apple around with the other hand. At the end, you should have a long piece of peel. This is quite a skill and very satisfying. You can eat the peel, curl it up, or dry it.

Handling Rejection

From the minute you start applying for jobs, you will be facing rejection in all its shapes and forms. Sadly, recruiters sometimes don't reply to emails or let you know why you have not been shortlisted. However, whether you receive a rejection by email, letter, telephone, or in person, you have to learn to deal with the fact that you have not achieved something that you might have wanted badly. Learning to handle rejection, processing the painful emotions, and moving on is what will help you apply for the next job with confidence and determination.

Practical exercise

FOCUS ON THE NOW

It's so easy to get sidetracked into either worrying about the past and regretting things that have happened or agonizing about the future (and seeing only disaster). Try and stay in the now as much as possible. Keep your attention focused on today, the things you need to do, and the tasks that need achieving. That doesn't mean not planning ahead, but stay focused on the now. Make a list of the things you need to do, with most difficult things first.

Boundaries at Work

Clean and clear boundaries are essential at work.
These apply to relationships with colleagues and employers,
which need to be appropriate, and also to doing the work itself.
Clear relationship boundaries means only talking about work at
work and being mindful about how much you share about
yourself. Clear work boundaries means not working way beyond
your hours, taking work home, or inappropriately sharing
information about your work with outside people. Being clear
about your boundaries will make you feel more trustworthy and
responsible and boost your confidence at work.

Digital Downtime

Whatever kind of work you do, it will probably involve new technology and screens. Many of us become slaves to our screens and can end up hurting our bodies and minds by not getting enough breaks. Then we watch devices on the commute home and go on the computer or watch TV or yet more screens once at home. We also check our cell phones constantly, up until bedtime. It is essential to have screen breaks and digital downtime to recover your equilibrium. Some people feel they must be contactable 24/7 and can never switch off. It is important to remember that you need breaks and downtime, as nobody is indispensable. Being confidently relaxed is very powerful.

Looking after Yourself at Work

We can persuade ourselves that we are indispensable and that it is necessary to work long hours. We might feel married to the business or workplace, working endlessly, including evenings and weekends, in the hope of gaining recompense or recognition. Yet we all need to take breaks, to have downtime, and to look after ourselves before, during, and after work. This includes the amount of alcohol and drugs we might consume in the evenings, weekends, or during lunches or meetings.

SITTING AWARELY

Take a moment to sit up in a chair or an armchair. Put your feet squarely on the ground, hip-width apart. Let your arms rest along the chair arms or along your thighs. Close your eyes. Feel the chair supporting your back, your shoulders, and your behind. Feel your feet on the ground. Take a deep breath in and breathe out slowly. Feel your hands along your thighs or the chair arms. Feel your back still held by the chair. Feel how solidly it holds you, how safe you are. Breathe in and out slowly, feeling supported. Do this for a couple of minutes before opening your eyes.

Practical exercise

CHAPTER SEVEN

Parenting Confidence

When deciding whether or not to have children,
many of us will wrestle with the following questions:

Would I make a good parent?
How would I know what to do?
What support would I have?
Have I got what it takes?
Shall I do it alone or with someone?
Can I afford it?
Am I patient enough?
Do I understand children?
How will I keep working?
Can I balance my life?
Can I curb my child-free lifestyle?

Psychological Influences

The decision to parent is something that both men and women wrestle with psychologically and emotionally. There is a concept of needing to be ready, or in other words mature enough, to have children. Many people feel concerned about starting their own families as they might have had negative experiences when younger. We may fear repeating the mistakes that our parents made and worry about damaging our own children. Climate change issues have also made many young people feel reticent about having a family, as the future may seem very uncertain.

What is Parenting Confidence?

One of the biggest issues people wrestle with
is their parenting confidence. This is a lack of confidence
in their personal qualities, their caring abilities, and fear of
responsibility. This is made more difficult if you have not had
a reliable parental role model, so people can swing
between either being too permissive or
over disciplinarian.

Self-Efficacy

"Self-efficacy" is a term coined in the 1970s by the psychologist Albert Bandura, about parenting confidence, meaning *"the belief in one's capabilities to organize and execute courses of action required to produce given attainments."* Further research by Lina Kurdahi Badr in 2005 defined it as *"the perception [parents] have about their ability to care for and understand their children."* Thus, parenting confidence is the perception you have that you can handle the many tasks associated with caring for a child.

Personality and Parenting

Lower self-confidence is linked to a lenient or permissive, or overreactive or harsh parenting style. Confident parenting is very much down to personality—being agreeable, emotionally stable, open to experience, warm and empathic, and even extroverted. The more anxious, uncertain, and overly cautious you are as a parent, the less confident you will probably be. Confident parents are:

Decisive without being domineering

Consistent without being rigid

Organized without being overcontrolling

Self-motivated without being isolated

Parenting Today

Parenting has never been more challenging. The pressures of modern life mean that many parents spend long hours working outside the home. Having to find childcare while trying to balance the demands of work and home life can be stressful. Many parents are living away from their own extended families, often in different cities or even countries, meaning that grandparents are not always on hand to help with childcare as they were in previous generations. Indeed, as retirement age increases many grandparents are still working and trying to juggle work and home life themselves. This can lead to parents, particularly new parents, feeling isolated and lacking in parenting confidence.

Good Preparation

In order to try and reduce stress, it is essential that prospective parents talk through (as much as possible) who will work, who will stay home, and how things like housekeeping will be done once a child arrives. Parents are often caught unprepared and then find themselves arguing over diaper-changing and dishwashing. Also, money is a key issue to discuss as openly and honestly as possible. This is especially important if one or both parents' income will be reduced, if there are debts to be dealt with, or if extra childcare will need to be paid for.

If the relationship flounders, it is also important to work out, as amicably as possible, what to do next. Using professional help at this point, such as a therapist or mediator, is a good idea to find a peaceful working solution. Parents need to remember that both partners will remain in a child's life (usually) until they die, so finding a working arrangement is good for everyone, particularly the children.

Self-Care for Parents

Parents need to remember to make time for each other—a date night once a month is a great idea. Use a trusted family member, friend, or experienced sitter to look after the children, or if that isn't possible have a date night at home once the children are in bed. Parents also need "alone time" to have a break every now and then. Looking after your needs is as essential as looking after the needs of your young one(s).

PARENT PICTURE

Use this exercise if you are not a parent but wish to be. Find a quiet space, either lying down or resting in a chair. Close your eyes and imagine a picture with a child. You are holding their hand and walking down a leafy lane with them, or cradling them in your arms singing a lullaby. "Watch" this picture in your imagination and enjoy seeing yourself in the parental role. Open your eyes and see how you feel.

SHOULDER ROLL

Try this if you are feeling tense. Sit up or stand, feet hip-width apart. Lift both shoulders up toward your ears, then roll them back and round. You might hear "clicks" as you do this. Do this six times, then change direction, rolling from the back to the front. Take a deep breath and blow it out.

Parenting Boundaries

Parents need to be dominant, but not domineering.
They need to be firm and boundaried, but not rigid. If you
are overcontroling, you can become a "helicopter parent."
hovering over your child's every move. Children need
independence within firm boundaries. A confident parent
trusts their own instincts and is not afraid to get
advice when needed.

Parents who are overly permissive, unboundaried,
and not very dominant create anxiety in their children.
No one knows what the rules are or how to operate. If you have
boundaries and are dominant (not tyrannical or aggressive),
then your child is free to be a child. They feel safe in expressing
themselves as they know you will know how to handle them.
When you are an emotional wreck or you flip-flop on decisions
or moods, your children don't know where they are and it can
make them anxious.

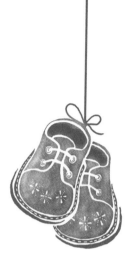

High Self-Efficacy Parenting
- *Willing to take on difficult tasks*
- *Willing to make a necessary effort to complete tasks and persevere*

Low Self-Efficacy Parenting
- *Greater self-doubt and high anxiety*
- *Avoids difficult tasks*

Competent Parenting
- *Warm and sensitive to the child's needs*
- *Engaged in their learning and development*
- *Have skills to respond to the child's needs*

Low Competency Parenting
- *Low self-esteem*
- *Often linked to substance and/or alcohol abuse*

Good Enough Parenting

Learning to be a "good enough" parent is important for the well-being of both parents and children alike. Instead of being a rigid disciplinarian or overly permissive, "good enough" parents are willing to follow a child's development and encourage their growth as an individual. These kind of parents will recognize their child's fears and difficulties and help them through them while recognizing people are not perfect. Struggles are normal and learning how to manage our fears and feelings is part of growing up. Parents need to be willing to work on themselves to manage their own mood swings, anger, fears, beliefs, and expectations.

All too often our own experiences of childhood can influence our children. If our experiences were positive, that's fine, but if they were negative this can be psychologically damaging. Parents who are willing to look at themselves and learn to improve their own parenting and develop a positive mindset may well bring up happy, confident children. Children model themselves on their parents, so the more confident we are in our own parental abilities the better it is for family life.

Calming exercise

MINDFUL TEA BREAK

Take a couple of minutes when you make your tea or coffee to notice exactly what you do and how you do it. Choose your favorite cup or mug. Pour the water and notice the steam. Watch the color of the tea grow in the cup or mug, or smell the coffee as it brews in a French press or cup. Then remove the tea bag, squeezing the tea out with awareness. Add milk (if you take it) and notice the changes in color. Sip and taste. Do nothing else while you do this but focus on the task.

How to Be a Good Enough Parent

No parent is perfect, and every parent will make mistakes. We all learn on the job, especially if we don't have family nearby. However, it is possible to become a better, more competent, confident, self-efficacious parent if you think about these three essential areas:

1. Care enough for your child to protect them from harm and establish clear physical and emotional boundaries about safety.
2. Make your interactions with your child supportive of their health on a developmental, emotional, and physical level.
3. Encourage and enhance your child's learning by facilitating their effective growth and development.

Alongside this, reward good behavior and try to minimize bad behavior. Always keep the channels of communication open —be available to your child and listen to them without criticizm, judgement, or overreaction. Also, make sure you look after yourself to be a good role model.

ENJOY BABY ANIMALS

Check out pictures of baby animals on your cell phone or in a magazine for a couple of minutes. Enjoyment of small animals boosts your endorphins and fills you with feel good emotions. If possible, stroke a baby cat or a dog, noticing their soft fur, their expressions, and the feeling of contact with another living thing.

Co-Parenting

You may be a parent to biological children or have step, surrogate, or adoptive children. If you are parenting with another person, confident parenting is a willingness to listen to your partner's views and beliefs, or to the things that are important to them, and work them out. All too often, people do not discuss their basic parenting beliefs or issues before they have responsibility for children, and then there are constant arguments and misunderstandings as a consequence.

LET GO IN DANCE

Calming exercise

In private, put on your favorite music and really let yourself go, like a child would. Dance around the room, be silly, wave your arms and legs, go with the beat. Enjoy mixing up moves and trying things out. It's great to move about, and it will oxygenate your blood, especially if you have been sedentary, static, or stressed for most of the day. Be as over-the-top as you like and enjoy the feeling of your body moving to sound.

When to Seek Help

Find a way to be clear with each other before you parent together or when you are parenting. Try not to battle over a child's head or turn differences into difficulties. Seek help from relationship or family therapists if things get too heated and entrenched. Remember that your parenting confidence will grow in time if you are willing to learn, to make mistakes, to look after yourself, and to seek support when you need it.

Calming exercise

CUSHION FLOP

Make a big pile of cushions. If you have a bean bag, big pillows, or duvet, pile them up, then flop onto them. Let the cushions hold your weight and completely relax. Get up and pile up the cushions again, into a mound, and flop down onto them again. Do this two or three times (safely of course), to give yourself a break.

CHAPTER EIGHT

Confidence for Life

Imagine feeling completely confident and self-assured. Just imagine yourself waking up feeling that it's great to be alive and that you are ready to face any challenges life may throw at you today. Imagine not worrying about what you said last night or whether you are up to tackling your to-do list today. Imagine going to work and facing those difficult people with ease, or making that presentation without notes, or feeling completely happy walking into any room.

Confident You

What would it be like to feel completely comfortable in your own skin, no matter who you've met and no matter what their reaction to you might be? Imagine feeling calm, collected, and relaxed about trying something new, taking a risk, asking someone out, persuading your boss for a promotion, or talking to a complete stranger. This chapter is all about mastering the techniques that will give you confidence for life, whatever the situation.

Self-Care for Confidence

There is nothing so confidence-building as feeling good about yourself when you meet people. This means attending to your bodily needs: your hygiene, your appearance, and your clothing are all important. This is not about spending lots of money and buying expensive fashion items or going wild in the cosmetics department—it's about treating yourself well and appropriately. Making sure you are clean, groomed, and appropriately dressed for the occasion is very important for your self-esteem and your self-confidence. If you are short on time, set your alarm a bit earlier to make time for that shower or teeth-brushing.

EVERYDAY CONFIDENCE BOOSTER

Empowering exercise

Stand with your hands on your hips, legs hip-width apart, head held high, chin jutting forward slightly. Make sure your head is held up straight, your shoulders are down, and your knees are soft. Think of Wonder Woman or Superman. Feel yourself in a powerful pose. Hold for a couple of minutes, then move your hands from your hips to point straight out at your sides and hold them there for a minute—count to sixty. Try expanding wider as you hold your arms out. Studies show that power poses release testosterone (the power hormone) into the bloodstream, and that holding this pose for two minutes diminishes cortisol, the stress hormone. Make this part of your daily self-care routine.

Attend to Yourself

Looking after yourself when you are ill or hurt, seeing a doctor when you need to, and getting treatment if you have an injury are all vital, but all too many of us put these things off. Value yourself and treat yourself like the precious being you are. When we suffer in silence, ignore symptoms, and tough out our injuries, we are being thoughtless about ourselves. A lack of self-care means a lack of compassion, and if we can't be compassionate toward ourselves then it will be hard for us to be kind to others. So it's worth taking the time to look after yourself and not be destructive or cavalier when you are hurt.

If we think of ourselves as sacred vessels, it becomes more difficult to put horrible, toxic things in our bodies. Smoking, junk food, alcohol, and drugs become anathema. You would not pour these things into a beautiful, fresh newborn, nor should you do it to yourself. These destructive habits ruin our well-being, make us operate under par, and are confidence-sapping. Going about our daily business with a hangover while feeling bad about our habits saps our self-esteem. Treating ourselves well is not about vanity; it is about treasuring the fact that we are alive.

Empowering
exercise

I'M ALIVE!

Find a private place to do this. Look in
a wall mirror if you can, or hold a hand
mirror up to your face. Smile and say *"I'm
alive!"* with joy. Repeat six times, getting
louder each time. You can also jump as you say
it or make a lively movement. See how this feels, stir
yourself up, celebrate being you.

Ten Steps to Confidence for Life

1. Remember that confidence can be learned. You can build your confidence step-by-step, and you will make progress if you try.

2. Work on your self-esteem. This is important for building your confidence. The more you like and value yourself, the easier it will be to be confident.

3. Learn from your mistakes. Don't let mistakes knock your confidence. See any difficulty as an opportunity for learning. It's important to lick your wounds, recover, and learn from the experience.

4. Prioritize self-care. Look after yourself to build both your self-esteem and self-confidence.

5. Get support when you need it. Reaching out and asking for help is essential, and there is no shame in getting therapy, coaching, or asking for help from friends or colleagues.

6. Act "as if" you are competent. By doing so, you will probably become confident in time (see page 152).

7. Build on what you know. Admit to yourself what you don't know but can continue to learn.

8. Ask for what you need. Find the courage to ask for what you need or want and take risks (not huge ones), and you'll get much further in the end.

9. Think positively. You will be much more confident and happy if you develop a positive mental attitude toward yourself and others.

10. Put yourself first. This is not about being selfish; it's about looking after yourself so you can look after others. Think of the oxygen mask in the plane that comes down for you before your loved ones: if you are not in good shape, you can't help others.

Learn to Be Good Enough

The current "cult of perfection" has meant that many of us feel unconfident because we recognize how imperfect we are. Being imperfect is being human, and that's fine. There is a tyranny about being perfect—physically, psychologically, emotionally, socially, financially, and so on. It's just not possible to be perfect. We are imperfect human beings and being "good enough" really is good enough. Let yourself off the perfection hook, and you will start enjoying being you.

Relaxing exercise

CHILD POSE COMFORTER

If you are feeling overloaded find a quiet corner. Kneel down and sit back on your heels. Put your arms out along the floor in front of you and bring your head onto your hands. Sit back farther on your heels and stretch out, head on your arms. Hold this position for a minute, then sit up again. Stretch up to the ceiling. Then go back into the pose for another minute. Relax.

Building Blocks for Confidence

Think of building your confidence like a wall.
Each brick is essential for a firm foundation. You can
build the wall any height, but whatever you do, you need
the foundation to be placed firmly on the ground to give you
balance, control, and power. Follow these "foundation"
steps to help build your confidence.

Know Yourself

Understanding who you are, how you think, what you like and don't like is vital, along with being honest about your own strengths and weaknesses. If you know you are moody, highly sensitive, or reactive, you will have to learn to manage yourself with others. Knowing this will equip you for handling yourself with people in all aspects of your life.

Assess and Take Risks

Confidence can make it easier to look a risk in the eye and be more adventurous. Taking risks (once assessed accurately) can lead to growth, which can also mean taking opportunities. The confidence to step out into the unknown may or may not succeed, but your new confident self will do it regardless of the outcome.

KEY TO SUCCESS

Take a couple of minutes to note down the skills or knowledge needed for an upcoming event. This might be a work presentation, a social engagement, or an exam. When you have your list, set about researching and taking on new information. This is a big step in building confidence for any task or situation. So, rise to the challenge and focus (or learn to focus) on what is essential for success.

Energizing exercise

Stop Self-Sabotage

It's a truism, but we often get in the way of our own success by sabotaging ourselves. Fear can make us get side-tracked. We want to do the job application, but we end up in the bar instead. We want to find a new partner, but we don't turn up for the date. We have to be truthful with ourselves whether we want to really succeed or not...and stop any self-sabotage.

Embrace Failure

For most of us, failure is a dirty word and stops us trying. Horrible memories of failed exams, lost jobs, bad dates, or terrible social encounters make us hide away. However, failure (in any form) is part of a learning curve. Having licked your wounds, pick yourself up, dust yourself off, and start all over again—wiser and better equipped to succeed.

VISUALIZE CONFIDENCE

Creative or positive visualization is vital in changing any negative mindsets regarding confidence. Envisioning successful encounters and experiences is part of the neural programming needed to change your behavior and thinking. As often as you can, take time to visualaize yourself as the confident person you wish to be. Imagine speaking at a conference without breaking a sweat or meeting new people without stumbling over your words. Really "see" yourself in the situation and note how you feel.

Visualization

BANISH NEGATIVE THOUGHTS

Repetitively thinking negative thoughts about yourself creates a downward spiral to nowhere. Yet, we can put our energy and focus on negative thoughts and thoroughly believe them. Stop these thoughts in their tracks and replace them with positive ideas and beliefs. Doing this regularly will build confidence and defeat the emotional, self-attacking drain of negative thinking.

ACT "AS IF"

Few of us are as confident as we want to be, so we have to start
somewhere. There are plenty of ways to start acting more
confidently, if we use our imaginations to change our behavior.
Acting "as if" we are confident will take us much further than
continuing to believe we are unable to take action. The next time
you are feeling less confident than you'd like, try acting "as if" you
are confident and calm.

Can-Do Attitude

Developing a "can-do" attitude can help you build your self-confidence. If you think "yes" and say "yes" to new challenges and pursue them, you will go farther than habitually saying "no." You may well assess the risk and say "no" to be sensible—great. But do you say "no" automatically and then wish afterward you'd tried? Develop a "can do" attitude, and you will get more confident with every experience (even with failures).

Take Baby Steps

Many people want to be confident overnight with an instant fix. It doesn't work that way. Confidence can be built, slowly but surely, with a series of baby steps, one after the other. If you are trying a new skill, seeking a new job, or finding a new partner, you will feel the usual human emotions of fear, anxiety, stress, and insecurity. However, try to take a baby step toward your goals regardless of these feelings—by all means acknowledge them but take a stab nonetheless.

CONFIDENT ME

Sit in a relaxed position. A high-backed chair or armchair is good. Or stand with your hands by your side. You can even do this in the bath. Say *"This is me"* to yourself with a smile. See how that feels. Repeat with a warm, confident tone, as if you were speaking to a familiar person you really like. See how you feel at the end. Continue with your day with this in mind—you're certainly good enough.

Confidence in Daily Life

Gaining confidence in daily life is all about being
able to live in the present, without constant nagging anxiety.
It is about being able to join in, make contact, and enjoy what
is on offer in the world. It is about knowing that you have a right
to be here and that you are entitled to be alive. It is not about
being arrogant or rude, putting other people down to
build yourself up, making ridiculous exaggerations,
or creating a false persona.

Maintaining Confidence

Confidence is quietly self-assured. It's sexy, calm, and it is like wearing an invisible cloak of power. To maintain confidence, remember to do the following every day:

- *Quit negative self-talk and self-criticizm.*

- *Think well about yourself.*

- *Develop a positive mental attitude of "I can" and "I will."*

- *Say "yes" and take risks.*

- *Treat yourself like the precious human you inherently are.*

- *Live in the present, not the past.*

Resources

Apps
Calm
Headspace
The Mindfulness App
Stop, Breathe & Think

Psychological Help
Mental Health America
www.mhanational.org/get-involved/contact-us

Warmline
www.warmline.org

National Alliance on Mental Illness
www.nami.org

Anxiety and Depression Association of America (ADAA)
www.adaa.org

The Trevor Project
www.thetrevorproject.org

Depression and Bipolar Support Alliance
www.dbsalliance.org

National Eating Disorder Association
www.nationaleatingdisorders.org

Meditation/Mindfulness
Be Mindful
www.bemindful.co.uk

Breathworks
www.breathworks-mindfulness.org.uk

Mind
www.mind.org.uk

Mindful
www.mindful.org

Samaritans
www.samaritans.org

Sleep
American Sleep Apnea Association
www.sleepapnea.org

Circadian Sleep Disorders Network
www.circadiansleepdisorders.org

Restless Legs Syndrome Foundation
www.rls.org

Narcolepsy Network
www.narcolepsynetwork.org

American Sleep Association
www.sleepassociation.org

Confidence
The Dove Self-Esteem Project
www.dove.com/us/en/dove-self-esteem-project.html

The Cybersmile Project
www.cybersmile.org

OneLove
www.joinonelove.org

Loveisrespect
www.loveisrespect.org

Books

The Mindfulness Journal by Corinne Sweet

The Anxiety Journal by Corinne Sweet

Full Catastrophe Living: How to Cope With Stress, Pain, and Illness Using Mindfulness by Jon Kabat-Zinn

About the Author

Corinne Sweet is an author, psychotherapist, psychologist, and broadcaster. She is the author of several popular psychology bestsellers, such as *Change Your Life with CBT*, *The Anxiety Journal*, *The Mindfulness Journal*, *How to Say No*, *Overcoming Addiction*, and *Stop Fighting About Money*. Corinne trained on BBC Radio 4's *Woman's Hour* and was a magazine and newspaper advice columnist and a *Big Brother* psychologist. She appears regularly on TV and radio, collaborating frequently with BBC Breakfast and BBC Radio Scotland. Corinne blogs regularly at www.corinnesweet.com.

Corinne is a psychotherapist at City Therapy Rooms (www.citytherapyrooms.co.uk) and Barnsbury Therapy Rooms (www.barnsburytherapyrooms.com) and is a registered British Association for Counselling and Psychotherapy member. She is a working single mom and has been a meditator and mindfulness user for over twenty-five years. She is also cochair of the Books Committee of the Writer's Guild of Great Britain.